This
Naure Storybook
belongs to:

_____

_____

For Aoife, Cora and Pádraig J.A.   For Charlie Peter Hill P.B.

First published 2019 by Walker Books Ltd, 87 Vauxhall Walk, London SE11 5HJ

This edition published 2020

2 4 6 8 10 9 7 5 3 1

Text © 2019 Justin Anderson   Illustrations © 2019 Patrick Benson

The right of Justin Anderson and Patrick Benson to be identified as author and illustrator respectively of this work has been asserted by them in accordance with the Copyright, Designs and Patents Act 1988

This book has been typeset in YanaR and Dink Scratch

Printed and bound in China

British Library Cataloguing in Publication Data: a catalogue record for this book is available from the British Library.

ISBN 978-1-4063-9198-5

www.walker.co.uk

Snow Leopard
Grey Ghost of the Mountain

Justin Anderson

illustrated by
Patrick Benson

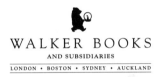

WALKER BOOKS
AND SUBSIDIARIES
LONDON • BOSTON • SYDNEY • AUCKLAND

The people who live among the high mountains of the Himalaya tell stories of a mysterious animal they call the "Grey Ghost".
They say that if you see it, you feel so happy and excited it's as if your soul is flying. But it is incredibly rare and hard to find, so to see one I'll have to be very lucky indeed...

My guide and I leave the village
behind and travel together,
up into the mountains.

As we climb, one slow step and then another, the slope gets ever steeper.

Suddenly, just in front of us, we see tracks in the snow. A line of pawprints that come from high up on the ridge.

Something moves in the rocks ahead.

My hands start to tremble. My heart is beating fast. But I must remain silent and still.

The grey ghost lives as high as 5,400 metres up in the mountains.
At this height the air has only half the oxygen we would normally breathe
so as you climb these peaks you get out of breath more easily.

There, not far away, is ...

A snow leopard!

Her coat is pale gold and silver-grey and painted with black rosettes.
It's easy to lose sight of her among the rocks: the rosettes look like
the shadows under stones and boulders and her pale belly
reflects the colour of the ground, breaking up her outline
and allowing her to disappear into the landscape.

Snow leopards can wander over an area of up to 1,000 square kilometres. This makes them very hard to track.

The snow leopard licks her paws. They are huge, as if she is wearing shoes that are much too big! They help her to spread her weight and travel across the deepest snow without sinking.

If you could get close enough to touch a snow leopard's fur, you would find 4,000 hairs tightly packed into the space beneath your fingertip. The thick fur growing on the soles of their feet helps keep them warm and stops them slipping on the icy rocks.

In the mountains the weather can change in an instant.

As the cold wind blows and fresh snow begins to fall, the leopard curls up, wrapping her tail around her paws like a cosy scarf. She buries her nose behind the thick spotted fur.

Snow leopards have the longest tail of any cat. Not only is it an amazing scarf, it helps them keep their balance when jumping between the rocks and when chasing after prey.

As the blizzard passes, the snow leopard shakes off the snow, stretches and yawns.

We watch quietly as she stops at an overhanging rock. She rubs against it with her cheek, turns her back, lifts her tail and squirts pee over the rock. It's a message for other cats to sniff out. This is how snow leopards stay in touch across the vastness of the mountains without ever meeting each other.

Snow leopard scientists call these messages "pee mails". They think that these smelly signals might tell other leopards the age and sex of the messenger, and even how long ago the message was left.

A clatter of hooves and the rattle of sliding rocks break the silence. Not all mountain animals are as quiet as the snow leopard!

Six ibex are crossing the slope below. The snow leopard has spotted them ... and she is hungry.

She sneaks in closer. With her camouflage coat, she melts into the mountainside.

Snow leopards hunt ibex, blue sheep, partridges, marmots and sometimes goats and yaks. They can leap nine metres in a single bound to catch their prey!

The muscles in her shoulders tense. She is ready to strike.

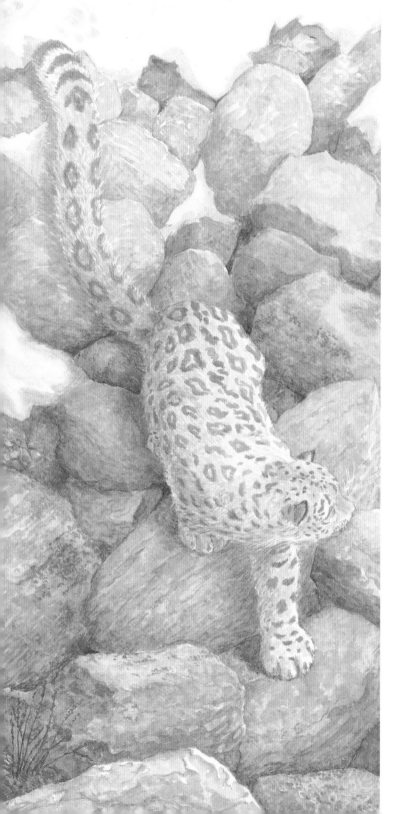

But something startles the ibex. They whistle in alarm and run away fast. The rocks they send tumbling sound like rain.

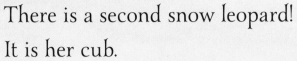

There is a second snow leopard!
It is her cub.

She is almost as big as her
mother, but still has a lot to
learn about keeping quiet
when mum is hunting.

The cub was born two years ago, blind and helpless in a secret mountain cave that her mother lined with warm fur from her own coat.

At seven days old, she opened her big blue eyes for the first time. Weighing less than a tin of beans, she grew fast on her mother's milk.

When they are born, snow leopard cubs have beautiful blue eyes — but as they grow older they change colour, becoming light green or grey. This is unusual: all other big cats have yellow or golden eyes.

At two months old, she tasted her first meat and a month later was ready to leave the cave. Since then she has followed her mother everywhere, learning how to survive – though soon she'll have to make her own way in the mountains...

A lot of snow leopards must share the same birthday, as almost all wild cubs are born in June and July.

But for now they snuggle up closely, nuzzling each other. The cub yawns and they begin to doze, soaking up what little warmth there is from the sun. Their tails curl together, as if they are holding hands.

I can't believe my eyes. I am watching two snow leopards. That is very lucky indeed!

During their first year of independence, young snow leopards travel up to 40 kilometres to find their own area to call home.

24

As the sun starts to sink, the leopards wake and slowly climb the mountain, beyond where we can hope to follow them.

For a second I think they have gone but then I see a tiny figure, right on the summit. It's the mother leopard. She begins to sing, her long haunting yowl echoing round the mountains, before fading on the wind. And then she is gone...

The Grey Ghost has disappeared.
Swallowed up by the silence.

More about snow leopards

On the IUCN's Red List of Threatened Species, snow leopards are listed as "vulnerable" – which means they are in trouble. Scientists think there may be as few as 3,920 left in the wild.

More and more people live up in the mountains, and many snow leopards are killed every year. Some are killed by farmers desperate to protect their animals and some by poachers looking to sell their beautiful fur, which is made into warm coats and hats.

Conservation groups have been helping local people in the mountain regions to protect them. In Ladakh in the Indian Himalaya (the setting for this book), there are many projects that aim to strengthen the bond between the mountain villagers and the leopards. In Hemis National Park, for instance, local people can earn a small living by making snow leopard toys and by taking tourists to see the animals in the wild.

But our changing climate is also a threat. In the Himalaya, temperatures are rising faster than the global average. The snow is melting, forcing the leopards ever higher up the mountains, giving them less space and making them more isolated. One prediction suggests that they could lose half of their mountain habitat in the next 50 years.

To find out more about saving snow leopards in Ladakh look up:

✳ Youth Association for the Conservation and Development in Hemis Park

✳ The Snow Leopard Conservancy of India Trust

Index

Camouflage 19

Coat 10, 19, 22

Cubs 21, 22–3,

Eyes 22

Fur 12, 14, 22

Hunting 19, 21

Paws 8, 12, 14

Pee 17

Prey 15, 19

Tail 14–5, 17, 24

Justin Anderson is a zoologist and film-maker with a passion for animals and wild places. He spent three years in Ladakh leading a BBC crew filming snow leopards for Planet Earth II. During that time his favourite adventures were riding a yak and hearing leopards singing in the moonlight. Justin says, "The first time I saw a snow leopard I was so excited I danced a little jig of joy!"

Patrick Benson says, "It was wonderful to be given the opportunity to illustrate Justin's story ... especially since I visited Ladakh nearly 30 years ago and fell in love with both the landscape and the people. I didn't see the fabled snow leopard, but I loved the idea that one might be watching me from high up above."

Note to Parents

Sharing books with children is one of the best ways to help them learn. And it's one of the best ways they learn to read, too.

Nature Storybooks are beautifully illustrated, award-winning information picture books whose focus on animals has a strong appeal for children. They can be read as stories, revisited and enjoyed again and again, inviting children to become excited about a subject, to think and discover, and to want to find out more.

Each book is an adventure into the real world that broadens children's experience and develops their curiosity and understanding – and that's the best kind of learning there is.

Note to Teachers

Nature Storybooks provide memorable reading experiences for children in Key Stages 1 and 2 (Years 1–4), and also offer many learning opportunities for exploring a topic through words and pictures.

By working with the stories, either individually or together, children can respond to the animal world through a variety of activities, including drawing and painting, role play, talking and writing.

The books provide a rich starting-point for further research and for developing children's knowledge of information genres.

Nature Storybooks support the literacy curriculum in a variety of ways, providing:
- a focus for a whole class topic
- high-quality texts for guided reading
- a resource for the class read-aloud programme
- information texts for the class and school library for developing children's individual reading interests

Find more information on how to use Nature Storybooks in the classroom at
www.walker.co.uk/naturestorybooks
Nature Storybooks support KS 1–2 English and KS 1–2 Science